SAGITTARIUS

SUN SIGN SERIES

Back C

D0822233

ALSO BY JOANNA MARTINE WOOLFOLK

Sexual Astrology

Honeymoon for Life

The Only Astrology Book You'll Ever Need

SAGITTARIUS

SUN SIGN SERIES
JOANNA MARTINE WOOLFOLK

TAYLOR TRADE PUBLISHING
LANHAM • NEW YORK • BOULDER • TORONTO • PLYMOUTH, UK

Published by Taylor Trade Publishing
An imprint of The Rowman & Littlefield Publishing Group, Inc.
4501 Forbes Boulevard, Suite 200, Lanham, Maryland 20706
www.rlpgtrade.com

Estover Road, Plymouth PL6 7PY, United Kingdom

Distributed by National Book Network

British Library Cataloguing in Publication Information Available

Library of Congress Cataloging-in-Publication Data

Woolfolk, Joanna Martine.
  Sagittarius / Joanna Martine Woolfolk.
    p. cm.—(Sun sign series)
  ISBN 978-1-58979-561-7 (pbk. : alk. paper)—ISBN 978-1-58979-536-5 (electronic)
  1. Sagittarius (Astrology) I. Title.
  BF1727.6.W66 2011
  133.5'274—dc22   2011003349

∞™ The paper used in this publication meets the minimum requirements of American
National Standard for Information Sciences—Permanence of Paper for Printed Library
Materials, ANSI/NISO Z39.48-1992.

Printed in the United States of America

I dedicate this book to the memory of
William Woolfolk
whose wisdom continues to guide me,

and to
James Sgandurra
who made everything bloom again.

CONTENTS

ABOUT THE AUTHOR

Astrologer Joanna Martine Woolfolk has had a long career as an author, columnist, lecturer, and counselor. She has written the monthly horoscope for numerous magazines in the United States, Europe, and Latin America—among them *Marie Claire*, *Harper's Bazaar*, *Redbook*, *Self*, *YM*, *House Beautiful*, and *StarScroll International*.

In addition to the best-selling *The Only Astrology Book You'll Ever Need*, Joanna is the author of *Sexual Astrology*, which has sold over a million copies worldwide, and *Astrology Source*, an interactive CD-ROM.

Joanna is a popular television and radio personality who has been interviewed by Barbara Walters, Regis Philbin, and Sally Jessy Raphael. She has appeared in a regular astrology segment on *New York Today* on NBC-TV and on *The Fairfield Exchange* on

CT Cable Channel 12, and she appears frequently on television and radio shows around the country. You can visit her website at www.joannamartinewoolfolk.com.

ACKNOWLEDGMENTS

Many people contribute to the creation of a book, some with ideas and editorial suggestions, and some unknowingly through their caring and love.

Among those who must know how much they helped is Jed Lyons, the elegant, erudite president of my publishers, the Rowman & Littlefield Publishing Group. Jed gave me the idea for this Sun Sign series, and I am grateful for his faith and encouragement.

Enormous gratitude also to Michael K. Dorr, my literary agent and dear friend, who has believed in me since we first met and continues to be my champion. I thank Michael for his sharp editor's eye and imbuing me with confidence.

Two people who don't know how much they give are my beloved sister and brother, Patricia G. Reynhout and Dr. John T. Galdamez. They sustain me with their unfailing devotion and support.

*We are born at a given moment, in a given place,
and like vintage years of wine, we have the
qualities of the year and of the season
in which we are born.*

CARL GUSTAV JUNG

INTRODUCTION

When my publishers suggested I write a book devoted solely to Sagittarius, I was thrilled. I've long wanted to concentrate exclusively on your wonderful sign. You are very special in the zodiac. Astrology teaches that Sagittarius is the sign of wisdom and expansion. Your sign represents freedom, adventure, and widening one's horizons. You have courage and high ideals and an open heart. Especially, you're known for your enthusiasm—you strive to get away from the mundane and aim for higher goals. Karmic teachers say you were specially picked to be Sagittarius because you were a philosopher and wise teacher in a previous life. But whether or not one believes in past lives, in *this* life you are Sagittarius, the passionate spirit of faith and the search for truth.

These days it has become fashionable to be a bit dismissive of Sun signs (the sign that the Sun was in at the time of your birth). Some people sniff that "everyone knows about Sun signs." They say the descriptions are too cookie-cutter, too much a cardboard figure, too inclusive (how can every Sagittarius be the same?).

Of course every Sagittarius is not the same! And many of these differences not only are genetic and environmental, but are differences in your *charts*. Another Sagittarian would not necessarily have your Moon sign, or Venus sign, or Ascendant. However, these are factors to consider later—after you have studied your Sun sign. (In *The Only Astrology Book You'll Ever Need*, I cover in depth differences in charts: different Planets, Houses, Ascendants, etc.)

First and foremost, you are a Sagittarian. Sagittarius is the sign the Sun was traveling through at the time of your birth.* The Sun is our most powerful planet. (In astrological terms, the Sun is referred to as a planet even though technically it is a "luminary.") It gives us life, warmth, energy, food. It is the force that sustains us on Earth. The Sun is also the most important and pervasive influence in your horoscope and in many ways determines how others see you. Your Sun sign governs your individuality, your distinctive style, and your drive to fulfill your goals.

Your sign of Sagittarius symbolizes the role you are given to play in this life. It's as if at the moment of your birth you were pushed onstage into a drama called *This Is My Life*. In this drama, you are the starring actor—and Sagittarius is the character you play. What aspects of this character are you going to project? The Sagittarian intelligence, optimism, and generosity? Its humanitarian outlook and ability to bring knowledge to others? Or its tactlessness, irresponsibility, self-indulgence, and moral arrogance? Your sign of Sagittarius describes your journey through this life, for it is your task to evolve into a perfect Sagittarian.

For each of us, the most interesting, most gripping subject is *self*. The longer I am an astrologer—which at this point is half my lifetime—the more I realize that what we all want to know about is ourselves. "Who am I?" you ask. You want to know what makes you tick, why you have such intense feelings, and whether others

---

*From our viewpoint here on Earth, the Sun travels around the Earth once each year. Within the space of that year, the Sun moves through all twelve signs of the zodiac, spending approximately one month in each sign.

are also insecure. People ask me questions like, "What kind of man should I look for?" "Why am I discontented with my job?" or "The man I'm dating is a Capricorn; will we be happy together?" They ask me if they'll ever find true love and when they will get out of a period of sadness or fear or the heavy burden of problems. They ask about their path in life and how they can find more fulfillment.

So I continue to see that the reason astrology exists is to answer questions about you. Basically, it's all about *you*. Astrology has been described as a stairway leading into your deeper self. It holds out the promise that you do not have to pass through life reacting blindly to experience, that you can within limits direct your own destiny and in the process reach a truer self-understanding.

Astrologically, the place to begin the study of yourself is your Sun sign. In this book, you'll read about your many positive qualities as well as your Sagittarius issues and negative inclinations. You'll find insights into your power and potentials, advice about love and sex, career guidance, health and diet tips, and information about myriads of objects, places, concepts, and things to which Sagittarius is attached. You'll also find topics not usually included in other astrology books—such as how Sagittarius fits in with Chinese astrology and with numerology.

Come with me on this exploration of the "infinite variety" (in Shakespeare's phrase) of being a Sagittarius.

Joanna Martine Woolfolk
Stamford, Connecticut
June 2011

SAGITTARIUS

NOVEMBER 22–DECEMBER 21

MICROSCOPIUM, AND TELESCOPIUM.

PART ONE

ALL ABOUT YOU

ILLUMINATING QUOTATIONS

"It's kind of fun to do the impossible."

> —Walt Disney, animator and film producer, a Sagittarius

"What if nothing exists and we're all in somebody's dream?"

> —Woody Allen, director and screenwriter, a Sagittarius

"I was wise enough to never grow up while fooling people into believing I had."

> —Margaret Mead, anthropologist, a Sagittarius

"I dream for a living."

> —Steven Spielberg, director, a Sagittarius

"My body has certainly wandered a good deal, but I have an uneasy suspicion that my mind has not wandered enough."

> —Noel Coward, playwright and composer, a Sagittarius

"When we remember we are all mad, the mysteries disappear and life stands explained."

> —Mark Twain, author and humorist, a Sagittarius

"You gotta love living, baby, 'cause dying is a pain in the ass."

> —Frank Sinatra, singer, a Sagittarius

YOUR SAGITTARIUS PERSONALITY

....

YOUR MOST LIKEABLE TRAIT: Optimism

....

The bright side of Sagittarius: Adventurous, optimistic, exuberant, open-minded, sincere

The dark side of Sagittarius: Extravagant, restless, irresponsible, careless, uncommitted

You're the sign of undiminished possibility, and are determined to experience all that you can extract from life. You're a conquistador who sees the next goal as a thrilling prize to capture and the next destination as a larger-than-life adventure. Sagittarius epitomizes being in motion—you're on a journey, whether this journey is physical, mental, or emotional. In the zodiac, you represent freedom, expansion, energy, and new ideas. You bring optimism and joy to others. The drawback is that unless you're moving through space like an arrow, you feel confined and dissatisfied. You have difficulty with stick-to-it-iveness and must learn to overcome procrastination and avoidance.

Ruled by Jupiter, planet of good fortune, you appear to breeze through life. You are Lady Luck's companion who seems always to be in the right place at the right time. Astrologers say you have the gift of providence—luck protects you. In work, friends, career, and money, a door opens just when you need it. Naturally, this makes for a cheerful and ebullient disposition. This is not to say you don't have dark moments of self-doubt, but emotional clouds roll over quickly. You are too interested in what's going to happen tomorrow to fret long about what went wrong today. The present is a means to the future—and you're eager to get on with the business of living, always sure that around the next bend of the road something wonderful is about to happen.

Not only does Jupiter's jovial energy light you, but Sagittarius is a Fire sign, and this radiant combination produces an expansive personality who cannot be confined. Independence is your guiding principle. You're the gypsy of the zodiac—a free, adventurous spirit who thrives on new ideas and a constant change of scene. The grass is always greener someplace else. Somewhere you picked up a chronic case of wanderlust, and you have no desire to be cured. What intrigues you is what waits just beyond the horizon.

Sagittarius, like its opposite sign, Gemini, wants to know. But whereas Geminis are happy to sample a new idea, Sagittarians will follow it as far as it will go. Sagittarius symbolizes the search for wisdom; it is the sign of the philosopher and the explorer.

High-spirited and congenial, you're a gifted conversationalist, a wonderful storyteller, and a born entertainer. You have wide-ranging interests—music, nature, philosophy, computers, technology, theater, animals—and enough energy to do six things at once.

Freedom is your most valuable possession. If it comes to a choice, you'll take a difficult path, accept less money, dispense with security, do anything, as long as you have to answer only to yourself. Your passion for liberty underlies all your other qualities. Prizing it as you do, you also willingly grant it to others. You don't meddle in other people's plans or interfere with what they think best for themselves, and you aren't possessive or jealous.

One of your finest traits is your honesty. You're upfront and straightforward, open-faced as a Danish sandwich, and always direct in your dealings. Your frankness makes you easy to deal with because one doesn't have to spend time figuring out the hidden significance of unspoken clues or nuances. There is no hidden significance. What you say is what you mean. And you're willing to tell all who ask exactly what you think of them—their lifestyle, hairstyle, choices, lovers, you name it. It's true you can be tactless, but your candid remarks are not meant to hurt. They spring from a desire to tell the truth, and people can trust what you tell them. It's ironic, though, that you yourself are rather thin-skinned and too easily hurt by a thoughtless action or careless rebuff. Beneath your spunky exterior lies a vulnerable and sensitive heart.

You're very good at friendship. Kind, generous, completely free of malice, you're the best pal in the zodiac. You like to do favors for others—literally, you'll offer the shirt off your back. It never occurs to you to say no or to begrudge giving your time, advice, or funds to others. Among the best gifts you give to people is your positive thinking; you help others to be more courageous.

The keyword in understanding Sagittarius is *possibility*. To be restricted or feel your choices are diminished is very depressing. You tend not to look at life as it is but as you want it to be. In many ways, you rebel against being a grownup. True, you've proven yourself strong in the face of setback, and crisis brings out the best in you. It's the "dailiness" of life that defeats you.

You lack staying power—you've got places to go, and you're not about to sign up for anything that confines you to one spot. Wherever you are, you keep an eye on the exit door. Often, before you're finished with one project, you're off to meet the next challenge. You have grand ideas for an adventurous career or carving out a utopian life or helping the world become a better place. Then you procrastinate, let others deal with the details, lose interest in a plan—and wonder why you're bogged down in the same place.

Astrology teaches that your superlative Sagittarian qualities (e.g., your expansiveness), when taken to extremes, create a chaotic life. You have a prodigality that wastes time, money, and certainly your extraordinary intellect. Instead of focusing your attention on practical plans with a chance of succeeding, you dissipate energy and brainpower on pursuits that are illusory. Thus, you keep yourself stuck while you blame the "system" for not allowing someone as brilliant as you to flourish and create.

You want the world to bend to your beliefs, and when this doesn't happen, you complain and sulk, grow cold and distant. Your agenda comes first, and, besides, in your mind, your priorities are right and true—they take the form of "ideals." You have a difficult time putting up with what you consider moronic rules and boring, limited people. When you're in this discontented state, you're a sorry sight. You feel cheated and abused, and droop with self-pity.

Still, Sagittarians are among the most likeable people in the zodiac. Yes, you can be extravagant and wasteful, even reckless and irresponsible. True, your life is full of forgotten appointments, missed deadlines, unfinished projects. True, your emotions can be shallow and your commitments almost nonexistent. Overriding everything, though, is the fact you're fun to be with. So what if you promise the moon and everyone knows you won't deliver? You know it too. There's nothing underhanded or secretive in the way you deal. You play with all your cards on the table.

Impetuous, buoyant, charming, you hitch your wagon to the merry-go-round of life and ride it with insouciant elegance.

THE INNER YOU

Like Scarlett O'Hara, your motto is, "Tomorrow is another day." Even in your darkest moods, you believe there's a light shining around the corner. Your confidence in the future is genuine, but you hate anything interfering with your plans. You have a hunger to experience life to its fullest—to travel, meet interesting people, and see things you've never seen before. Anything new sparks your interest. In fact, you'll usually say yes to a suggestion without weighing its merits simply because it lifts your spirits. And while you're not exactly a moody person, you are high-strung and can become irritable when you start to get bored. You may think no one cares about you or understands you when you're feeling this way, but luckily your belief that you're someone special always sees you through.

HOW OTHERS SEE YOU

People like your sense of humor and your buoyant presence. No matter what goes wrong, you're ready with an upbeat explanation and forecast for the future. You're also the first to volunteer help; colleagues and friends appreciate your willingness to do favors.

People like your frankness, although sometimes they think you can be too blunt and that you put your foot in your mouth too often. To some you seem fickle and undependable, perhaps a bit too detached emotionally. In general, you're viewed as an unpredictable, independent spirit.

GUARD AGAINST:
Becoming the Conceited Thinker

You have a tendency toward arrogance and being condescending to others. You need to develop the patience to *listen* rather than doing all the talking yourself. You can easily fall into being the self-important loudmouth who gets into arguments over the finer points of the subject. You feel you know best, that you're smarter and more informed, and you're fond of your own opinions. You believe your own judgment is the true path, and you can be irritatingly close-minded (which coexists with your openness toward gaining new knowledge).

This tendency of "knowing more" is part of the Sagittarian predisposition toward doing things to excess. You want more of whatever it is you want. You need to learn the difference between need and greed. Fondness for good food can lead to gluttony; wanting to be a leader leads to being power hungry. You're dissatisfied. Your restless intellect can lead you to become the perennial student who keeps pursuing an education to prepare for a career that never gets underway. Taking spontaneity to the extreme, you'll jump into a project, trip, or enticing invitation, without any preparation. You seek instant gratification, and then you're soaring onto something else.

Yours is the sign of expansion, but you need to learn that living without boundaries does not open up expansion but creates chaos—and chaos will ultimately enslave you.

YOUR GREATEST CHALLENGE: To Take Responsibility

The Sagittarian spirit loves the idea of limitless possibilities, a tricky concept that can easily tip into foolish impulsiveness. In your exuberance, you have a way of overpromising and overextending, and living in denial. You may mean what you promise when you say it, but that was back then; as the time comes around to deliver, you've bounded off into something more exciting. Delivery and deadlines feel like detention centers, and you don't want to be incarcerated. You dislike having to answer to authority and being tied down. The problem is your fear of being "tied down"—to a job, a schedule, a mate—makes you run from commitment. And in doing this (in the curious way life works) you create your own prison of discontent and loneliness, unconnected to the people and projects you would most love and find most joy in.

Another problem with one's head being in the clouds is it leads to poor choices and bad judgment. When lacking discipline, you lack a sense of direction. Many Sagittarians are dabblers and procrastinators and experts in the art of rationalization. Always there are reasons—you have a challenge to meet, you don't want to be on a treadmill, you need to take this detour so you can be on your way somewhere. But your unwillingness to grow up traps you; you're ambushed by childish whims you mindlessly follow. Your scattered mind goes round and round, talking about big dreams but stuck in the shallows. It's ironic that your mad flight toward freedom limits your freedom.

Your greatest challenge is to tap into your high purpose and do the committed work necessary to reach your goals. The ancients taught that freedom and discipline are inseparable; you cannot have one without the other. With discipline you can be a great achiever. You were born with vision, and when you back up your dreams with control and strictness, you will access that higher power within yourself.

YOUR ALTER EGO

Astrology gives us many tools in our lives to help manage our struggles and solve problems. One of these tools is to reach into your opposite sign in the zodiac—your "polarity." For you, Sagittarius, this is Gemini, sign of communication, information, day-to-day dealings, and short journeys. The sign of Gemini represents interaction with the immediate environment. Its planetary ruler, Mercury, holds sway over the exchange of news, self-expression, mental activity, and being in transit from one place to another.

Like you, Geminis possess curiosity, intellectual quickness, and a high degree of sociability—but they are not intent on breaking free of the constraints of today or finding their higher purpose, nor do they have your "missionary" tendencies. Geminis focus on what's current. They have scintillating mental energy and strong links to others, and they find reward in expressing themselves in their careers and being in contact with people. The busier they are, the more crammed their schedules, the greater number of activities with friends and colleagues—the more Geminis feel fulfilled.

In many ways, Gemini and Sagittarius have much in common. Both are Mutable signs (the quality of restless movement). Both need time to learn, independence to discover, and space to create. The big difference is that Gemini's *raison d'être* is to connect and communicate, whereas yours is to experience what's over the horizon and find a larger universe in which to operate—in essence, to fly the coop and get out.

Your unrealized dreams and the impatience you feel about being confined cause great discouragement. And when you fixate on how others are petty and small-minded as opposed to your being more honest and intelligent, what you do is alienate yourself. You can spare yourself much internal conflict by adopting more of Gemini's interactive approach, its focus on relating, and its here-and-now attitudes.

Keep up your connections; stay in touch. Communicate—whether you're talking about feelings or just the weather. Plan a social activity. Set an immediate goal (a small one will do) and concentrate on finishing that project. Work on a hobby that uses your hands (e.g., playing an instrument, painting, needlecraft, model trains). Any activity that centers you on the present will counteract your Sagittarian tendency to live in your dreams and waste time in the now. Concrete, immediate accomplishments keep you from getting stuck in pie-in-the-sky ventures that block your true creative output.

In turn, Gemini has much to learn from you. Gemini is intensely concerned with what others think, keeping up appearances, and being the cleverest person in the room. Gemini can also be amazingly superficial and insincere. Sagittarius is more concerned with greater achievements and making what you do count for something. You have penetrating intelligence that doesn't skim the surface. Your ambitions will leave a legacy. Gemini needs to tap into your integrity and courage, your sense of the drama of life. You're able to see the deeper potential in ideas and also in people. You know life holds more importance than scrambling around, trying to stay busy, trying to impress. If Gemini could believe this, it would find itself far less confused and spinning in place.

SAGITTARIUS IN LOVE

Sagittarius is the sign of lust for life. You pulse with verve and sensuality, and like all Fire signs (Aries, Leo, Sagittarius), are at your most vibrant when you're in love. You're drawn to the excitement of romance and have an exuberant, spontaneous approach to relationships. Since your attitude in general is enthusiastic and positive, being in love intensifies these glowing feelings. You are a true romantic in the sense that you believe in love for love's sake rather than for money or social position. You have an open heart and, especially when you're young, a tendency to fall in love at first sight.

But Sagittarius is also the sign of mental exploration, and for a relationship to last, it needs to be an adventure. Your free spirit finds domesticity boring and routine the kiss of death—and you rapidly tire of anyone who thinks on a scale smaller than you. You feel suffocated by a partner who does not respect your freedom, and the more a lover tries to hold you, the quicker you try to escape. If he or she attempts to corral your independence, you quickly look for unfenced pastures. A true relationship to you is a contract that allows each to be who you really are, so chances improve for the union to last if your lover has a life of his or her own.

At the start of an affair, you're the charming pursuer. Sagittarius the Archer loves the chase. Even if you're the female, you have an inviting, enticing, approachable directness that sends a clear sexual message. Neither male nor female Sagittarian is aggressive, but both have a straightforward frankness about the game of love. Indeed, being refreshingly honest is a Sagittarian trademark. You hate whatever is artificial, pompous, or pretentious, and prefer the easygoing approach in all things. On a date, for example, Sagittarius is as happy with an informal lunch at an outdoor café as with a grand dress-up dinner.

Your exploratory nature may lead you to have a number of early sex experiences. You have a secret predilection for the sex-with-a-stranger syndrome and are often drawn to encounters that begin quickly in an exotic setting and have a passion-in-the-moment edge (e.g., a tryst on a train speeding through Europe, wild sex with a new lover on a beach in Barbados).

You don't always perceive the consequences of romantic entanglements. Basically, you're more mental than emotional, and each new love is a learning experience. You're stimulated by the chase, the thrill, but you don't necessarily go deeply into the relationship. You can detach rather easily and move on into the future (which of course is better than the present). You don't take into account that when a romance is over it may leave behind a trail of wounded feelings. If an old lover harbors resentment, you're genuinely surprised.

You're definitely not domineering, but in a sense you do dominate the relationship because it's always on your terms. You are the perfect playmate but only as long as you find the game worth playing. You're not one to make the best of a bad bargain. If you're unhappy, you won't resign yourself or compromise or try to work things out. You'll just walk out.

Sagittarians are hard to pin down emotionally. You don't want to get bogged down in messy entanglements or anything that ties you down. You've got places to go, and you're not about to sign up for anything that keeps you in one spot. The way to stay unfettered is to shy away from emotion. Sagittarians rarely talk about their feelings—they talk about what they *think* about their feelings. Time and again, Sagittarians are bewildered when their romantic partners ask for more passion and feeling. Far less than natives of other signs, you don't need a relationship to fill you. You need it to *enhance* your experience of life, but not to complete you.

Still, you can be a romantic and sensual lover—you're as exuberant in lovemaking as in every other area of your life. You want sex to be truthful, genuine, very impulsive. You are also insistent on being sexually pleasured as much as pleasing your lover. You need variety; making love the same old way is boring. Your lover has to have an open mind and body, delighted to sample the entire menu of erotica—with an appetite for the feast. The thing is you don't consider love to be an experience like the movies tell it. You're passionate but not intense. Your great quality is enthusiasm, a sense of sheer enjoyment

What confuses lovers is you believe a love affair should be a grand passion and a grand *friendship* rolled into one. You need both in a relationship—plus plenty of communication. You want someone with a sense of humor, intelligent, open, full of life, who matches your high energy level. You want to share travel, exciting activities, interesting food, the great outdoors. And it would be nice if he or she loved animals.

Unless every necessary ingredient is in the relationship, you're not interested in anything long-term. You'll tarry for the fun and laughter and then move on. Even in the most perfect love affair, you have much more on your mind (your myriad interests and endeavors) than just the relationship.

There does come a time, though, when you do fall deeply in love, and then you're unshakably loyal. You're a unique combination of romantic partner, fun companion, and deeply sensitive friend. For Sagittarius, happiness is not a fixed goal—it's a way of traveling—so the fact you can explore life together becomes the most exciting, romantic journey in the world!

TIPS FOR THOSE WHO WANT TO ATTRACT SAGITTARIUS

You won't have trouble striking up a conversation. Sagittarians are interested in almost anything. When they've talked themselves out on their favorite subjects, they'll decide *you're* a fascinating conversationalist!

Ask about their work, their friends, books they have read, and their reactions to a current news event. If you happen to like animals or outdoor sports, you are already halfway home with Sagittarius.

There is a fine line between taking an interest in their interests and prying. Don't overstep that boundary. Sagittarians are very wary of anyone who might be trying to corner them. If talking about generalities gives you the feeling that you're sliding rapidly over ice, don't worry. Matters will improve on better acquaintance. You may discover, in fact, that your problem is trying to ignore the direct, sometimes overly frank inquiries that Sagittarians will make. When they get to know you, they like you to share confidences with them or ask for their advice.

Sagittarians like outdoor dates: dancing under the stars, open-air concerts, picnics at the beach, skiing or sailing outings. They usually avoid large parties or too-close quarters because they cannot bear to be hedged in or confined. Never infringe on their freedom. Never let your emotional needs intrude on their private lives. And you'd be wise not to put too much stock in their promises. Their words are writ on water.

Enjoy being with Sagittarius, but don't think you've signed a lifelong contract, because Sagittarius doesn't think so. And don't look back with regret when it's over. Sagittarius won't.

SAGITTARIUS'S EROGENOUS ZONES:
Tips for Those with a Sagittarius Lover

Our bodies are very sensitive to the touch of another human being. The special language of touching is understood on a level more basic than speech. Each sign is linked to certain zones and areas of the body that are especially receptive and can receive sexual message through touch. Many books and manuals have been written about lovemaking, but few pay attention to the unique knowledge of erogenous zones supplied by astrology. You can use astrology to become a better, more sensitive lover.

The special erotic areas for Sagittarius are the hips and thighs. Sagittarians like to be touched and caressed in these places. Both males and females enjoy kisses, nibbles, and delicate fingering along the inside of the thighs and around the hips.

Try giving Sagittarius a rubdown of the upper legs with warm body oil. He or she is sure to find it sexually arousing. Use circular motions on the hips and vertical strokes on the thighs.

Another erotic massage technique is to begin stroking the outside of Sagittarius's thighs with four fingers while exploring the inside of the thighs with your thumbs. Stroke upward toward the genitals. Then stroke the inside of the thighs with the palm of your hand. Switch to using fingertips or fingernails and just barely touch the skin. Stroke upward along the inner thigh so that your fingertips touch the thighs and your knuckles brush against the genitals.

By this time erotic sensations are shooting up the spine of your Sagittarius.

SAGITTARIUS'S AMOROUS COMBINATIONS: YOUR LOVE PARTNERS

SAGITTARIUS AND ARIES

Both of you share a similar approach to sex (you make the most of *every* opportunity). Add to this a mutual love of the outdoors and a fondness for socializing, and it's easy to see why you two get along so well. You're also intellectually well suited: You both have a wide range of interests and love to talk about them. Sagittarius is more philosophical about problems than Aries, who becomes more personally involved. Basically, you are two highly individual people whose idiosyncrasies mesh. Psychologists would say you mirror each other, and each helps the other to understand him- or herself better. The keys to your success as a couple are to work together toward common goals and not take advantage of the trust between you. There is a question mark about your combustible tempers, for arguments are heated. However, they're short-lived and the making up will be fun. An excellent match.

SAGITTARIUS AND TAURUS

Taurus wants to run things, but you won't be controlled. You need change, variety, and adventure, and this proves irritating to steady, disciplined, home-loving Taurus. Taurus approves of tried-and-true ways of doing things, while Sagittarius will try anything. Taurus sees Sagittarius as an escapist who won't accept responsibility, and often your daredevil spirit is deflated by Taurus's conservatism, which is a major downer. Also, as a blunt Sagittarian, you say what you think at the drop of a hat, and this brings Taurus's temper to a slow simmer. There are money problems, as well, since Sagittarius gambles today while Taurus hoards for tomorrow. At the beginning of your affair, a glimmer of hope resides in your passionate eroticism, but this only lasts until your first clash over lifestyle, friends, money, and aspirations. As a romantic duo, you have a short future.

SAGITTARIUS AND GEMINI

Both of you are restless, adventuresome, imaginative, and fun-loving. No other opposite signs in the zodiac enjoy each other more than you two. There will be shooting stars in the bedroom for a while, but when the fireworks fizzle the bickering begins. You both have bright minds, but Sagittarius is outspoken and bossy, while Gemini likes to poke verbal fun. The problem is you are two self-involved people with a tendency toward agitation and dissatisfaction. Neither is comfortable with emotions or getting too close, so while your relationship can skim along cerebrally for a time, you two don't have a real heart connection. As a couple, you're easily bored and need the stimulation of friends and social life to distract you. Too rootless and discontent to settle down, you both eventually succumb to the siren call of other interests, other loves. But parting should be amicable.

SAGITTARIUS AND CANCER

Cancer's sensuality and romantic imagination intrigue you, who like to experiment sexually. But your Sagittarian nature is both venturesome and cerebral while Cancer is cautious and emotional, and you two will never understand each other. You can't supply Cancer with the security and stability it yearns for, and you can't endure Cancer's moodiness and jealousy. You're blunt and straight-talking, and without being aware of it, you wound sensitive Cancer at every turn. Sadly, from the very start Cancer is hooked on your energy and vitality, and keeps crowding into the space you want to keep between you two. This becomes highly claustrophobic, and you quickly look for escape. When you seek outside stimulation away from home, Cancer nags and whines and tries to hold on tighter. You two are far better off as friends, and even then the homebody and the vagabond have little in common.

SAGITTARIUS AND LEO

Exciting times are ahead for you two ardent lovers. Self-confident Leo holds the key to unlocking your deeper Sagittarian passions, and your sex life together is a sensuous adventure. The two of you also enjoy travel, meeting new people, and each other's company.

Your laughter uplifts Leo, and Leo's extroverted nature seamlessly meshes with your expansive outlook. Leo loves freedom as much as you do, so there won't be problems with jealousy or possessiveness. You share an underlying friendship that supports without crowding. Leo and Sagittarius can be competitive, but this brings out the best in both, and happily each of you has an eye for financial opportunity. A bonus in your relationship is that with your Sagittarian charm, you have the lightness of touch necessary to cope with Leo's monumental ego—Leo is like putty in your hands. A grand mating.

SAGITTARIUS AND VIRGO

Immediately, Virgo is drawn to your spontaneity and charisma, and Virgo's classiness appeals to you. But Virgo is also shy and reticent and can't take the initiative, which makes you think Virgo is prudish. Early in your affair you two can manage some sexual combustion, but it's fleeting. Both of you do have intellectual leanings, so you may end up having some interesting conversations in bed. Elsewhere, Virgo looks for order and simplicity, whereas you look for excitement and new experiences. Your view is skyward, but Virgo is earthbound. Virgo needs to be needed, but you prize self-sufficiency. Virgo wants a long-term commitment; Sagittarius has to be free to roam. Your slapdash ways irritate meticulous Virgo. When Virgo carps and criticizes, this is sometimes a way of showing it cares, but you will never understand that. Little bodes well in your relationship.

SAGITTARIUS AND LIBRA

You are charmed by Libra's artistic, elegant, easygoing nature, and Libra is fascinated by your lust for adventure. Libra is more romantic than you; otherwise, the sexual harmony is delightful. Libra casts a tolerant eye on Sagittarian frolicking, and may even slow you down, for Libra knows how to turn on sensual charm and can be exceedingly seductive. In other areas, you have lovely compatibility as well. Together you enjoy hobbies, cultural events, new people, interesting places, and learning about different cultures. You both have life-of-the-party personalities, and, if anything, Libra is even more social than you. A slight wrinkle is each has spendthrift tendencies, so someone must learn to watch the pennies. Also, Libra enjoys its home as a luxurious showplace, and Sagittarius prefers the outdoor life. But Librans are artists at working out such problems.

SAGITTARIUS AND SCORPIO

Immediately, Scorpio is captivated by your cheery energy, and you're more than tantalized by Scorpio's dark passions, especially its murky secretiveness. (Closed systems always tempt you to find out more.) But just as immediately, Scorpio tries to clip your wings and keep you in a cage. Brooding, pent-up Scorpio just can't deal with your open, ebullient, outspoken personality. Your far-roaming interests constantly make Scorpio jealous. Romantically, this is a volatile combination. Sagittarius is playful about sex, and you find Scorpio's intense, dominating passions too much to cope with. Soon your inclination is to fly. You're also quick-tempered

_23

but cool quickly, while Scorpio's anger seethes until it erupts in fury. The essential problem is Scorpio is all about power and control, and Sagittarius absolutely will not bend to any authority. A temperamental, difficult union.

SAGITTARIUS AND SAGITTARIUS

Some astrologers believe the only fit mate for a Sagittarian is another Sagittarian. You two do seem perfectly suited: two independent, freedom-loving roamers. Your friends certainly enjoy you, for you're likely to be the fun ringleaders of your social group. However, as love partners, your exciting, chaotic, eventful relationship is too unpredictable to suit either of you. The dynamic between you is that both think each should understand the other and give the other all the latitude you need. But these unrealistic expectations breed disappointment and a pervasive resentment. Two Sagittarians have a tendency to bring out the worst in each other. Both get caught up in a plethora of impractical plans and unfinished projects. Finances tend to be chaotic. Each of you remains uncommitted, and you have so many outside interests that you inevitably drift apart.

SAGITTARIUS AND CAPRICORN

If only you could work this out, you two could really give each other what you need. Capricorn can use your buoyant outlook, and you definitely can benefit from the strength and stability of Capricorn. At the beginning, your sexual coming together is delightful, but unfortunately it's doomed not to last. Capricorn's demands can't be satisfied by your lighthearted approach to love. Both of you have high aspirations in life, but your approaches are totally different. Capricorn wants to climb to the top of the mountain; Sagittarius wants to fly over the top. Your frank, outspoken nature is sure to rile Capricorn's sensibilities. Capricorn is restrictive, a loner, known for its dour outlook. Sagittarius is venturesome, sociable, and expansive. Capricorn is cautious with money and concerned with appearances—and you are neither. Both of you should look elsewhere.

SAGITTARIUS AND AQUARIUS

Your minds are what first attract each other, for both of you are curious and a bit eccentric. Aquarius is innovative; Sagittarius loves to experiment. Aquarius delights in your spontaneity, and you admire Aquarius's humanitarianism. You share a zest for adventure and a forward-looking viewpoint. You both like to explore possibilities to the fullest and are idealists about love and life. You also fit each other's foibles well—neither wants to be hemmed in and therefore neither will try to tie down the other. There'll be imaginative fun in the bedroom, and together you're likely to find out things to include in *The Joy of Sex*. Astrologically, Sagittarius and Aquarius are the signs of friendship. You're sparkling companions who enjoy the *journey*; you genuinely like each other. True emotional intimacy may be slower to develop—but prospects are wonderful for the long haul.

SAGITTARIUS AND PISCES

Pisces is drawn to your Sagittarius life force, and you're attracted to Pisces's spirituality. But you need a pal and Pisces needs a dream lover—and neither of you can help the other. Your naturally buoyant spirits are anchored by Pisces's dependency and timidity. You have many outside interests, and Pisces's self-sacrificing bent does allow you to get away with neglectful behavior, but this out-of-balance relationship is essentially a brief encounter. Highly emotional Pisces is looking for more than a no-strings sex partner, whereas restless, freedom-loving Sagittarius is looking for nothing but. Unfortunately, what you do have in common is that each is divorced from the realities around you. Pisces is a dreamy escapist, while you just want to move on to your next big adventure. Bedroom high jinks keep things going for a while, but your affair quickly sinks into a quagmire.

YOUR SAGITTARIUS CAREER PATH

With lucky Jupiter as your planetary ruler, success seems to follow you. An opportunity arrives just when you need it, and, unlike many people, you're born with a sense that whatever fate puts in front of you, you can handle. You have brains and imagination and humor, and certainly you're unusually versatile. Your accepting attitude about new ideas and utilizing the uncommon gives you a leg-up in the workplace. You don't allow yourself to get stuck in the same old, same old.

Since your Sagittarian nature is to fight confinement, and sameness bores you, you may very well take a number of jobs before you find the one that unshackles your creativity. Even then, you'll continually make plans for improving or changing or moving on to the next thing.

One thing that keeps you independent and inventive is that you're not fixated on monetary success the way, say, a Capricorn or Taurus person might be. You don't need millions and millions; you'd be happy with just a great beach house and an ever-renewing checking account. For you, the project itself is far more important than fame and power. Indeed, in your mind, power is *freedom* (to pick and choose, to say no). You love your liberty.

Another quality that adds excitement is you enjoy the element of risk. You perform best when there's something really important at stake, when you're down to your last chance to win, when it's now or never.

This makes you a good entrepreneur. While others are still considering a prospect, you're acting on it, and you'll take chances others won't. Of course, it helps that you're blessed with foresight and clear thinking. Sagittarius is a visionary sign. You're interested in the future, not the past.

In addition, you have an irresistible knack for making friends of colleagues and associates, which means you have support. People trust you. Your contagious good cheer instills confidence, and further, your sharp intellect lying behind your gregarious exterior is very apparent.

This quick intelligence is fueled by your primal instinct, which is to *know*. You try to learn from everything you undertake and everyone you meet. Thus, what you're best at always involves a fresh idea and dealing with people. Plus, you look for challenges. The Sagittarius Arrow, symbol of your sign, stands for high aims—your aspirations are beyond the mundane. You're an explorer, and also an idealist. Your bent is always toward making a difference in the world, bringing enlightenment.

Professions you're suited for are the law, teaching, and medicine. You could have a career in politics or be an advocate for special causes, such as the environment or animals rights. Your ability to write and speak well shows you can make your mark in journalism, publishing, TV, and communications. Because you love animals, you can get involved in training them or becoming a veterinarian. The travel industry strongly appeals, and the Foreign Service could make use of your talents.

Your best quality in a career—as in every other part of your life—is your optimism. You believe in your lucky star. Any action is better than none, you're convinced, and so you plunge ahead, willing to take what comes, positive that all will turn out well.

Still, despite your ebullience and sterling talents, your issues are about your need to fly outward. And in the curious way the universe works, these issues hold you back. Overexpansiveness in both your ideas and your style frequently forces you back down to earth with a disillusioning thud. No matter how much you want to believe, hard facts sometimes puncture your pipedreams and you have to deal with reality.

You also have a problem with perseverance. The long haul is not your thing. Your talent is for getting things started, and then you'll abandon a job and move on in order to avoid routine. You love meeting a challenge, but once the challenge is met, a lot of the zest goes with it.

Because you're more interested in what's beyond rather than in what's in front of you, you have a tendency to be slapdash and sloppy with details. You're like a restless schoolchild impatient to get out of the classroom and onto the playground.

When you're in your scattered-mind mode, you talk and talk about big plans that never get underway. This ensures not only that the plans will not see the light of day, but that you, yourself, become a boring person. This downward-spiraling pattern of big talk but no action can definitely keep you mired in the same place.

Yet you have everything you need to propel you forward— enormous resilience, spunk, willingness to trust yourself, and super-sharp intelligence. Especially, you believe in possibility. The trick is to know the difference between possibility and *im-*

possibility. You must learn that structure creates freedom, and discipline brings independence. When you're focused and channeled, when you make productive use of your time and stick with the project to the end, you can master anything you touch.

SAGITTARIUS AND HEALTH: ADVICE FROM ASTROLOGY

Physical movement is the key to your good health. More than for any other sign, exercise is crucial. Sagittarius represents the freedom to leap ahead with enthusiasm—and for you, stagnation will bring on lethargy, weight gain, depression, and disease. Because you have a lively personality as well as an active mind, any routinized or confining exercise quickly bores you. In every season, you're happiest in the fresh air partaking of exhilarating recreational adventures. Being Jupiter-ruled, you're an enjoyer inclined to overindulge in the pleasures of food and drink. You must be vigilant about your dietary habits and careful about excess drinking. Your liver is your sensitive place, and alcohol is very damaging to it. You're usually on the go and tend to exhaust yourself; you need to schedule periods of complete relaxation.

Advice and useful tips about health are among the most important kinds of information that astrology provides. Health and well-being are of paramount concern to human beings. Love, money, or career takes second place, for without good health we cannot enjoy anything in life.

Astrology and medicine have had a long marriage. Hippocrates (born around 460 B.C.), the Greek philosopher and physician who is considered the father of medicine, said, "A physician without a knowledge of astrology has no right to call himself a physician." Indeed, up until the eighteenth century, the study of astrology and its relationship to the body was very much a part of a doctor's training. When a patient became ill, a chart was immediately drawn up. This guided the doctor in both diagnosis and treatment, for the chart would tell when the crisis would come and what medicine would help. Of course, modern Western doctors no longer use astrology to treat illness. However, astrology can still be a useful tool in helping to understand and maintain our physical well-being.

THE PART OF YOUR BODY RULED BY SAGITTARIUS

Each sign of the zodiac governs a specific part of the body. These associations date back to the beginning of astrology. Curiously, the part of the body that a sign rules is in some ways the strongest and in other ways the weakest area for natives of that sign.

Your sign of Sagittarius rules the hips, the thighs, and the liver. In human anatomy, the hips and thighs represent locomotion and volition, and it should not be surprising that most Sagittarians are active people who love freedom, fresh air, sunshine, and the great outdoors. Physical activity is a must; you will stagnate and become ill if you don't get enough exercise.

Both men and women tend to have long, well-shaped legs. You are graceful, coordinated, and well developed and are often described as having a buoyant walk. Indeed, walking is a favorite form of relaxation and exercise.

Though you're usually lean and slender in your early years, you have a tendency to put on weight as you get older. In Sagittarian women, the weight unfortunately seems to settle on the hips and thighs.

Sagittarians are likely to incur injuries and ailments of the hips and thighs. Your upper legs are the first part of the body to tire and weaken when you're under strain. Often, you have chronic aches in the hips and thighs, and are susceptible to fractures, sprains, and bruising in this area. You're vulnerable to sciatica, gout, hip disease, and sometimes lameness.

Sagittarius's ruling planet, Jupiter, governs the liver. In addition, recent astrologers have traced Jupiter's influence on the pituitary gland. The pituitary, known as the "master gland," regulates hormone production and physical growth. You tend to have an active, sensitive liver that instantly suffers from overuse of alcohol. You are also susceptible to hepatitis.

With a minimum amount of care, however, you enjoy a long, healthy life. There are more octogenarians born under Sagittarius than under any other sign.

DIET AND HEALTH TIPS FOR SAGITTARIUS

Proper diet is important for on-the-run Sagittarians. A poor diet heavy in fats, starches, and alcohol places an extra burden on your sensitive liver and makes it harder for you to sustain a high energy level.

Sagittarius's cell salt* is silica, which strengthens the nervous system, keeps the connective brain tissue healthy, and prevents numbness in fingers, legs, and feet. Deficiency of this mineral results in lank hair, dull skin, and sores and receding of the gums. Best sources for the silica that Sagittarius needs are the skins of fruits and vegetables, raw salads, green peppers, figs, prunes, strawberries, pears, apples, potatoes, oats, the husks of grains, whole-grain cereals, and egg yolks. Foods that particularly do not agree with you are fats, gravies, cream, butter, candy, and chocolate. You should go very easy on alcoholic beverages to avoid damage not only to the liver but also to the skin, which coarsens and ages under the effects of liquor. To keep your weight at an optimum level, you should eat a high-protein diet, with lots of broiled poultry and fish, fresh vegetables and fruit (such as brussels sprouts, beets, tomatoes, asparagus, plums, cherries, oranges, and lemons), eggs, skim milk, yogurt, brown rice, and whole wheat.

Sagittarians need constant mental stimulation, which can lead you to overwork and overplay. More than most people, you have to have recreation and exercise, but moderation is the keyword. You

*Cell salts (also known as tissue salts) are mineral compounds found in human tissue cells. These minerals are the only substances our cells cannot produce by themselves. The life of cells is relatively short, and the creation of new cells depends on the presence of these minerals.

should avoid the blistering effects of sun and wind, for your skin is apt to be quite thin and tender.

Other good tips: You should drink lots of pure water, avoid smoking tobacco (which constricts blood vessels), eat four mini-meals a day rather than three large ones, and be careful when walking, riding, or participating in sports. Injuries to the hips and thighs are common among Sagittarians.

In general, you're healthy and optimistic, recuperate quickly from illness, and keep your good looks and sparkling smile well into old age.

THE DECANATES AND CUSPS OF SAGITTARIUS

Decanate and *cusp* are astrological terms that subdivide your Sun sign. These subdivisions further define and emphasize certain qualities and character traits of your Sun sign Sagittarius.

WHAT IS A DECANATE?

Each astrological sign is divided into three parts, and each part is called a *decanate* or a *decan* (the terms are used interchangeably).

The word comes from the Greek word *dekanoi*, meaning "ten days apart." The Greeks took their word from the Egyptians, who divided their year into 360 days.* The Egyptian year had twelve months of thirty days each, and each month was further divided into three sections of ten days each. It was these ten-day sections the Greeks called *dekanoi*.

---

*The Egyptians soon found out that a 360-day year was inaccurate and so added on five extra days. These were feast days and holidays, and not counted as real days.

Astrology still divides the zodiac into decanates. There are twelve signs in the zodiac, and each sign is divided into three decanates. You might picture each decanate as a room. You were born in the sign of Sagittarius, which consists of three rooms (decanates). In which room of Sagittarius were you born?

The zodiac is a 360-degree circle. Each decanate is ten degrees of that circle, or about ten days long, since the Sun moves through the zodiac at approximately the rate of one degree per day. (This is not exact because not all of our months contain thirty days.)

The decanate of a sign does not change the basic characteristics of that sign, but it does refine and individualize the sign's general characteristics. If you were born, say, in the second decanate of Sagittarius, it does not change the fact you are a Sagittarian. It does indicate that you have somewhat different and special characteristics from those Sagittarian people born in the first decanate or the third decanate.

Finally, each decanate has a specific planetary ruler, sometimes called a subruler because it does not usurp the overall rulership of your sign. The subruler can only enhance and add to the distinct characteristics of your decanate. For example, your entire sign of Sagittarius is ruled by Jupiter, but the second decanate of Sagittarius is subruled by Mars. The influence of Mars, the subruler, combines with the overall authority of Jupiter to make the second decanate of Sagittarius unlike any other in the zodiac.

FIRST DECANATE OF SAGITTARIUS

November 22 through December 1
Keyword: Honesty

Constellation: Ophiuchus, the Serpent-Holder, who as a child vanquished his serpent enemies. Ophiuchus symbolizes victory over adversity.

Planetary Subruler: Jupiter

Jupiter, planet of wisdom, is both your ruler and subruler, which accentuates lofty ideals and a love of knowledge. You look for experience and adventure. You want to deepen your understanding of life and are usually a student of human nature. People know they can trust what you tell them, for you are open and aboveboard. In addition, you have a special talent for pleasing others by what you say. You believe strongly in freedom, in the right of each person to choose an individual pathway. Because you have such wide-ranging interests, you may find it hard to commit yourself completely to a marriage or love affair. Emotional discord is extremely distressing to you; you strive to surround yourself with harmonious relationships.

SECOND DECANATE OF SAGITTARIUS

December 2 through December 11

Keyword: Drive

Constellation: Sagitta, the Arrow that killed the eagle who fed upon Prometheus. The Arrow symbolizes the destruction of evil in its path.

Planetary Subruler: Mars

Mars, planet of initiative, combines with Jupiter's expansiveness to give you a courageous and generous nature. You have the rare gift of being able to influence and inspire others. Often, the kindnesses you show have a much greater impact than you know. Your life is usually geared toward a goal; your real respect is for achievement. You are dependable, efficient, and thorough when you undertake to do a job. At times, you may be discouraged, but the face you show to the world is one of humor and strength of character. You are a person of fierce independence; you want to do things your way, though you will try not to step on any toes. In love, you may seem detached, but you are devoted and loyal.

THIRD DECANATE OF SAGITTARIUS

December 12 through December 21
Keyword: Intuition
Constellation: Ara, the Altar of Dionysus (Bacchus). Christian astronomers called it the Altar of Noah. Ara symbolizes unity and triumph.
Planetary Subruler: Sun

The Sun, which stands for pride and vitality, joins forces with beneficent Jupiter. Together they give great magnetism to your personality and a charming talent for making people laugh. Often, your profound intellect is hidden under a social and gregarious exterior. Gifted with intuition and insight, you have great capacity for learning and discovering deeper meaning. You enjoy travel and meeting new people, for you want to widen your experience. The world of teaching or writing beckons to you. You have a refined and elegant nature that responds to art and beauty. In love, you are passionate and impulsive. You tend to fall head over heels quickly, but these crushes fade away just as quickly.

WHAT IS A CUSP?

A cusp is the point at which a new astrological sign begins.* Thus, the cusp of Sagittarius means the point at which Sagittarius begins. (The word comes from the Latin word *cuspis*, meaning "point.")

When someone speaks of being "born on the cusp," that person is referring to a birth time at or near the beginning or the end of an astrological sign. For example, if you were born on December 21, you were born on the cusp of Capricorn, the sign that begins on December 22. Indeed, depending on what year you were born, your birth time might even be in the first degree of Capricorn. People born on the very day a sign begins or ends are often confused about what sign they really are—a confusion made more complicated by the fact that the Sun does not move into or out of a sign at *exactly* the same moment (or even day) each year. There are slight time differences from year to year. Therefore, if you are a Sagittarian born on November 22 or December 21, you'll find great clarity consulting a computer chart that tells you exactly where the Sun was at the very moment you were born.

As for what span of time constitutes being born on the cusp, the astrological community holds various opinions. Some astrologers claim cusp means being born only within the first two days or last two days of a sign (though many say this is too narrow a time frame). Others say it can be as much as within the first ten days or last ten days of a sign (which many say is too wide an interpretation). The consensus is that you were born on the cusp if your birthday is within the first *five* days or last *five* days of a sign.

*In a birth chart, a cusp is also the point at which an astrological House begins.

The question hanging over cusp-born people is "What sign am I really?" They feel they straddle the border of two different countries. To some extent, this is true. If you were born on the cusp, you're under the influence of both signs. However, much like being a traveler leaving one country and crossing into another, you must actually *be* in one country—you can't be in two countries at the same time. One sign is always a stronger influence, and that sign is almost invariably the sign that the Sun was actually in (in other words, your Sun sign). The reason I say "almost" is that in rare cases a chart may be so heavily weighted with planets in a certain sign that the person more keenly feels the influence of that specific sign.

For example, I have a client who was born in the evening on December 21. On that evening, the Sun was leaving Sagittarius and entering Capricorn. At the moment of her birth, the Sun was still in Sagittarius, so technically speaking she is a Sagittarian. However, the Sun was only a couple hours away from being in Capricorn, and this person has the Moon, Mercury, and Venus all in Capricorn. She has always felt like a Capricorn and always behaved as a Capricorn.

This, obviously, is an unusual case. Generally, the Sun is the most powerful planetary influence in a chart. Even if you were born with the Sun on the very tip of the first or last degree of Sagittarius, Sagittarius is your Sun sign—and this is the sign you will most feel like.

Still, the influence of the approaching sign or of the sign just ending is present, and you will probably sense that mixture in yourself.

BORN NOVEMBER 22 THROUGH NOVEMBER 26

You are Sagittarius with Scorpio tendencies. You are high-strung and excitable and may be known as a colorful personality. You are also intelligent, versatile, and forward-thinking. Life is full of activity for you. Because you dislike being alone, you surround yourself with people and projects and sometimes spread yourself too thin. You know how to spot an advantage and how to make yourself the center of attention. You have good psychic powers and an ability to probe into other people's minds. In love, you are passionate but changeable.

BORN DECEMBER 17 THROUGH DECEMBER 21

You are Sagittarius with Capricorn tendencies. You are genial and good-natured and have charming social manners. You are also ambitious, know how to take on responsibility, and are thorough when doing a job. Since you have both imagination and a strong sense of self, you like to work without interference from others. People sometimes look to you for advice, since your quick mind can zero in on important matters. You have a sensitive nature and a capacity for loving deeply. You do not always make wise decisions in love, however.

YOUR SPECIAL DAY OF BIRTH

NOVEMBER 22

You're more stubborn, emotional, and sensual than many Sagittarians. You have a distinct imaginative flair you can turn into financial gain. You'll always be somewhat restless in relationships, and need a lover who can see into your soul.

NOVEMBER 23

You have a generous heart, and people are drawn to your intelligence. Yet you struggle with dark thoughts that you're failing. Your destiny, though, is to achieve in the public eye. In love, you tend to be too forgiving of a partner's bad behavior.

NOVEMBER 24

Original and inventive, you were a precocious child who always knew your life would be unusual. You want to be rooted but also to fly away, and in time you will satisfy both impulses. In love, you're a passionate romantic who has difficulty with ordinariness.

NOVEMBER 25

You're full of initiative and not designed to be poor. You're forceful in your opinions, though you try not to give offense. In creative work, you have originality and an eye for detail. Love happiness is elusive, but you will open your deepest self to someone true.

NOVEMBER 26

You're not meant for overnight success, yet when it arrives, people will think it was overnight. You have star power, but need to anchor your vivid imagination with practical ideas. In love, you offer passion and friendship, and must have your own space.

NOVEMBER 27

You're a natural. Whatever you touch you're good at, so in order to achieve greatness you must learn to focus on your passion. Publicly you're charismatic, and privately a worrier. In love, you're impulsive, but after painful early lessons, you'll choose wisely.

NOVEMBER 28

You're highly intuitive—your heart reads people better than your mind. But you need to use both in relationships, especially career alliances. You're gifted at writing and communicating. Romantically, you have powerful allure and are a very sensual lover.

NOVEMBER 29

You have a rich inner life and are also an intellectual virtuoso. In your work, your people-charm is a strong advantage; you do well in one-on-one dealings. In love, if you're careful not to give more than you take, you'll be adored by one special person.

NOVEMBER 30

Your combination of elegance and determination makes you different. You're a rebel with high ambition and strong ethics. Lovers especially are drawn to your magnetism, but you're fussy about to whom you give your heart and body. You're extremely loyal.

DECEMBER 1

You have versatile talents—and the work you're best at is the one that's a "happy accident." You're daring in following gut instinct rather than advice. In love, you're passionate and seem always to end up the strong one who takes care of your lover.

DECEMBER 2

You yearn to see new worlds and do imaginative deeds. Progress is slow at first, but you will fulfill many of your dreams. You're gifted creatively, and never let on how sensitive you are to criticism. Your faithful heart will find great joy in love.

DECEMBER 3

As self-critical as you are, others see a master craftsperson. You have an innate sense of design and how to work with people's agendas; therefore, in a career, you'll create a bold venture. In love, you're a grand romantic who follows your heart (sometimes foolishly).

DECEMBER 4

You're careful and cautious about small decisions, but in important things like ambition and making money, you're an extravagant risk-taker. In love, especially, you seek adventure and in your youth tend to make choices that astonish others. Later on, you find true love.

DECEMBER 5

You're adored for your zaniness and willingness to give anything a shot. Half of you is an adventurer, and the other half wants an ordered life. You need a deeply intimate love-mate and also a supportive family, which can create a dilemma of divided loyalties.

DECEMBER 6

You drive yourself hard and are a perfectionist. At the same time, you're a maverick drawn to unusual work and an unconventional life. You're markedly independent. You need a lover with a tolerant eye and also able to give you abiding friendship.

DECEMBER 7

You're a benign warrior who lives life on your terms. Emotionally you're elusive, and intellectually eccentric, yet people are devoted to you for your generous heart. In romance, the one who falls in love with you will truly love your complexities.

DECEMBER 8

Though you're private, you have an alluring public persona. You were actually born to be a performer (even when you say no), and in your lifestyle will break out of a mold. Love can be a rocky road because you get into power struggles. Your lesson is to develop patience.

DECEMBER 9

You're high-spirited and zany, yet oddly you have a poetic nature. You notice shadings in relationships, and see into people's secrets. In work, you always attract attention from an audience. In love, you want to be "captured" but have issues around trusting.

DECEMBER 10

You have inner beauty others see as a radiant sweetness. You're intelligent, creative, multitalented, and a hard worker. Your problem is self-doubt. In love, therefore, be careful about becoming the sacrificer and settling for less than you're worthy of.

DECEMBER 11

You seem to run on your nerves and caffeine. Quick-thinking and a fascinating talker, you're skilled at leading groups of people. In romantic affairs, you display assurance you don't always feel; when you let a lover see your vulnerable side, you find real intimacy.

DECEMBER 12

You appear fearless and, indeed, have the courage to follow your instincts. The good thing is you were born with nobility and will take risks to do the right thing. In love, be wise in your choices, for to your detriment you're drawn to being a rescuer.

DECEMBER 13

To you you're a pussycat, but you are dominating, obsessive, caring, and passionate (not a stereotypical Sagittarian). You're at your best when you have a crisis to handle. Your flirtatious manner attracts many, but you need a mate with "class."

DECEMBER 14

Gregarious and giving, you're the first one others turn to when they need advice. You're a learner and creator, and you need work that takes you off the beaten track. Romantically, you yearn to be swept away but will choose someone who is more practical than you.

DECEMBER 15

Life will always put you in unusual situations in which you affect others deeply. You're spontaneous, brave, and (though you'll laugh) heroic. In relationships, you give shelter. In romance, you need passionate love and would rather be alone than settle.

DECEMBER 16

You're a quick study and you "get" things in a flash. At times, you're psychic and never wrong about others' motives. You have a vibrant style in dress and decorating. You need to be loved and pampered, and are a sexy lover, but relationships tend to be chaotic.

DECEMBER 17

You have wonderful intelligence, and a magical way with words. When you can discipline yourself, you turn out exceptional work. You're capable of loving strongly, but you put your lover on a pedestal. Then, disappointingly, the scales fall from your eyes.

DECEMBER 18

You're elegant and magnetic, yet you feel you don't fit in. This is because you're different—you're a "dreamweaver" who's supposed to follow a unique path in creative work and how you live. You will find a love mate to fill you and help you reach your potential.

DECEMBER 19

People can be intimidated by your sharp wit, but you're truly a sweetheart with a giving heart. You have a knack for making lucky connections socially and at work. In love, spontaneous passion is your thing—only someone superintelligent will get you to settle down.

DECEMBER 20

Whatever you touch has originality—you concoct inventive plans and have the gumption to see them through. Secretly, you may feel you're a plodder, but in reality you are a genius. You're also a wild romanticist; in time, you'll find the one who can feed your hungry heart.

DECEMBER 21

You're ahead of the curve in ideas, choices, style, and creative work. You have the courage to stay true to your taste—though you do have trouble staying within a budget! In love, you tend to give too much, but when you learn how worthy you are, you'll find a soulmate.

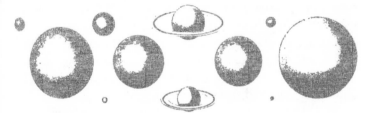

YOU AND CHINESE ASTROLOGY

With Marco Polo's adventurous travels in A.D. 1275, Europeans learned for the first time of the great beauty, wealth, history, and romance of China. Untouched as they were by outside influences, the Chinese developed their astrology along different lines from other ancient cultures, such as the Egyptians, Babylonians, and Greeks from whom Western astrology has its roots. Therefore, the Chinese zodiac differs from the zodiac of the West. To begin with, it is based on a lunar cycle rather than Western astrology's solar cycle. The Chinese zodiac is divided into twelve years, and each year is represented by a different animal—the rat, ox, tiger, rabbit, dragon, snake, horse, goat, monkey, rooster, dog, and pig. The legend of the twelve animals is that when Buddha lay on his deathbed, he asked the animals of the forest to come and bid him farewell. These twelve were the first to arrive. The cat, as the story goes, is not among the animals because it was napping and couldn't be bothered to make the journey. (In some Asian countries, however, such as Vietnam, the cat replaces the rabbit.)

Like Western astrology, in which the zodiac signs have different characteristics, each of the twelve Chinese animal years assigns character traits specific to a person born in that year. For example, the Year of the Rat confers honesty and an analytical mind, whereas the Year of the Monkey grants charm and quick ability to spot opportunity.

Here are descriptions for Sagittarius for each Chinese animal year:

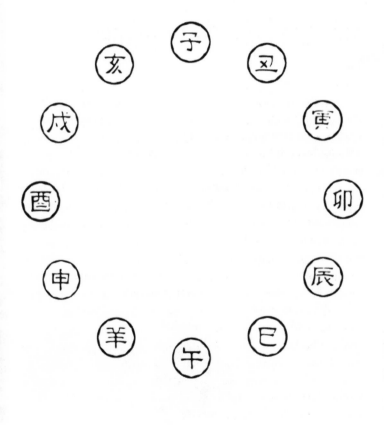

Years of the Rat

1900	1960	2020	2080
1912	1972	2032	2092
1924	1984	2044	
1936	1996	2056	
1948	2008	2068	

The Chinese are fond of the inventive, intelligent, charming Rat—and you, born in the Year of the Rat, are said to be ambitious, outspoken, multitalented, and have great personal flair. Rat allure and activism blend beautifully with your Sagittarian creativity and adventurous outlook. Your nimble, analytical mind can get you out of any jam and seize any opportunity. You're quick to take advantage; this is a good thing, for you're an initiator. (Rat years mark new beginnings.) As a Sagittarian Rat, you're born with panache, known for your adroit social touch. It's true you can also be a meddler and grumbler, but you get away with a lot because of your humor. You're enormously sentimental and, in love, a passionate giver who will easily spoil the one you care for. Your nature is to look out for yourself and those you love. Compatible partners are born in the Years of the Monkey, Pig, Rat, and Snake.

Years of the Ox

1901	1961	2021	2081
1913	1973	2033	2093
1925	1985	2045	
1937	1997	2057	
1949	2009	2069	

The West thinks of the ox as dull and plodding, but the Asian Ox is a creature of elegance and originality. The Ox inspires confidence with its level-headedness and high intelligence. Ox equanimity grounds the Sagittarian propensity for spacing out and not dealing with the now. The combination of stick-to-it-iveness (Ox) and being a visionary (Sagittarius) makes you an artist and achiever. You're both placid *and* fiery, and you have refined taste. Your particular genius is to take an outrageous idea and fashion it into something solid and worthy. Granted, your precise mind can become impatient and picayunish, and you do have a pronounced stubborn streak. This fixed tenacity is especially evident in love. You're fervently loyal as well as a passionate, sensuous lover, and sometimes are too self-sacrificing. Compatible partners are born in the Years of the Rabbit, Rooster, Monkey, Pig, and Snake.

IF YOU ARE SAGITTARIUS BORN IN THE YEAR OF THE TIGER

Years of the Tiger

1902	1962	2022	2082
1914	1974	2034	2094
1926	1986	2046	
1938	1998	2058	
1950	2010	2070	

The Tiger symbolizes strength and magnificence, and to Buddhists the power of faith. Born in the Year of the Tiger, you command attention. Tiger boldness plus its rebellious spirit merge with your Sagittarian exploratory nature to emphasize the courage to be different. You have big ideas and aren't afraid to pursue them, and you make audacious lifestyle choices. Indeed, you need major challenges, for you grow stagnant and depressed if your talents are caged. You do have a way of rubbing people the wrong way when you're hotheaded and hasty. But you're a grand risk-taker who inspires. In romantic affairs, you combine passion and erotic sensuality with possessiveness, though you yourself tend to have a wandering eye unless you're totally smitten. You are, however, capable of great love. Compatible partners are born in the Years of the Rabbit, Dog, Dragon, Monkey, Tiger, and Pig.

IF YOU ARE SAGITTARIUS BORN IN THE YEAR OF THE RABBIT

Years of the Rabbit

1903	1963	2023	2083
1915	1975	2035	2095
1927	1987	2047	
1939	1999	2059	
1951	2011	2071	

The Asian Rabbit (or, in countries such as Vietnam, the Cat) is buoyant, articulate, ambitious, and creative. Born in the Year of the Rabbit, you're a thinker and artist, blessed with far-reaching imagination. Blending Rabbit elegance with Sagittarian audaciousness produces a special theatrical pizzazz. You definitely have a gift for captivating people. As a Sagittarius Rabbit, you're also considered lucky financially, although money by itself is less interesting than expressing yourself. You want to be rewarded for being talented. Some may call you vain and a dilettante, but usually because they're envious of your physical beauty that gets so much attention. You certainly attract lovers. However, romance does not always run smoothly because you long for perfect bliss yet are sexually provocative. Compatible partners are born in the Years of the Goat, Dog, Dragon, Snake, Horse, and Monkey.

IF YOU ARE SAGITTARIUS BORN IN THE YEAR OF THE DRAGON ㊞

Years of the Dragon

1904	1964	2024	2084
1916	1976	2036	2096
1928	1988	2048	
1940	2000	2060	
1952	2012	2072	

In China, the Dragon has mythic stature, for it symbolizes immortality and connotes a special destiny. If you're born in the Year of the Dragon, you're meant to live a life that has greatness—in your work, creativity, and impact on others. Dragon charisma combined with Sagittarius's visionary intelligence makes you a passionate innovator. Your free spirit is never trapped by petty rules, and you're a role model for how much an independent thinker can achieve. With your taste and flair, even if you came from reduced circumstances, people assume you were born into wealth. Sometimes you can be too outspoken and downright irritating in your perfectionist stubbornness. Love brings out your best qualities of honesty and loyalty, though you're a grand romantic often disappointed when the champagne bubbles go flat. Compatible partners are born in the Years of the Rabbit, Goat, Monkey, Snake, and Tiger.

Years of the Snake

1905	1965	2025	2085
1917	1977	2037	2097
1929	1989	2049	
1941	2001	2061	
1953	2013	2073	

Unlike the Western snake with its reputation for evil, the Asian Snake is revered for its elegance and artistry. It is a treasured companion to the Goddess of Beauty and the Sea. The Snake has subtlety, wisdom, glamour, and goodwill—qualities that make your Sagittarian *joie de vivre* even more glowing. You're fluent in speech, an excellent problem-solver, and brilliant at dealing with groups. Your honesty shocks and delights, and you're wonderfully persistent (you won't be stopped by negative people). Ancient sages taught that the Sagittarius Snake is both exciting and dark— you have an arresting magnetism and a deep inner life. Romance brings out your complications: you're sexually restless, possessively jealous, and passionately intense. Your love affairs tend to be rollercoaster rides. Compatible partners are born in the Years of the Rabbit, Rooster, Dragon, Horse, Ox, and Rat.

IF YOU ARE SAGITTARIUS BORN IN THE YEAR OF THE HORSE

Years of the Horse

1906	1966	2026	2086
1918	1978	2038	2098
1930	1990	2050	
1942	2002	2062	
1954	2014	2074	

The Chinese Horse has magnificence and immense power. In Asia, the Year of the Horse is considered so influential that pregnancies are planned around it. Horse qualities of drive, speed, and ardor ignite your Sagittarian daring, and you're capable of galvanizing people and ideas into one-of-a-kind projects. You also have an outrageous sense of fun. As a Sagittarius Horse, you put your own stamp on all you touch. Horse years promote striking out on one's own, and for you the theme of zooming through life as a revolutionary is ever present. Add to this your unusual mix of caring and pragmatism, and you're the one who can make real change happen. You're a romantic, and the arena of love is filled with passion and soap-opera drama. Early on you'll sow your wild oats, but when you commit your wild heart to someone, you are faithful. Compatible partners are born in the Years of the Rabbit, Rooster, Goat, Horse, and Snake.

IF YOU ARE SAGITTARIUS BORN IN THE YEAR OF THE GOAT

Years of the Goat

1907	1967	2027	2087
1919	1979	2039	2099
1931	1991	2051	
1943	2003	2063	
1955	2015	2075	

In the West, the goat has a humorous, often salacious connotation, but the Chinese Goat is highly intelligent, gifted, graceful, and accomplished. The Goat is drawn to everything first-class and rarified. Goat qualities of creativity and excellent judgment underline your Sagittarian ability to see larger potential in an idea. You're a craftsperson and artisan, and whether your work is in business or the arts, you take meticulous care to make it perfect. Your Sagittarian propensity for being an acute observer works perfectly with Goat sensitivity—people come to you for explanations of their own behavior. It's true you yourself must fight insecurity. This is at the root of your fussbudget ways and your capriciousness (changing your mind because you're unsure). In love, you're inwardly shy and outwardly aloof, but you warm up quickly. Indeed, you have abundant sensuality, though you do nitpick and nag. Compatible partners are born in the Years of the Rabbit, Dragon, Horse, Monkey, and Pig.

IF YOU ARE SAGITTARIUS BORN IN THE YEAR OF THE MONKEY

中

Years of the Monkey

1908	1968	2028	2088
1920	1980	2040	2100
1932	1992	2052	
1944	2004	2064	
1956	2016	2076	

The charming and amusing Monkey is a beloved figure in Asia—and, in mythology, the cheerful companion to the God of Sailors on long voyages. The Monkey is quick-witted, vivacious, and inventive, as well as mischievous. Indeed, the Monkey has a devious side. Monkey cleverness and nimbleness (in thought and action) add kinetic energy to your Sagittarian enthusiasm and especially your curiosity. As a Sagittarius Monkey, you're an ambitious *inventor*. You may start with the tried and true and then spin a concept into something never done before. People are taken with your humor and the touch of the rogue you possess, but don't like it when you're not honest. In love, you're changeable. You fall in love in an instant but find true intimacy hard to sustain. You particularly adore the merry chase at the start of an affair. Compatible partners are born in the Years of the Rabbit, Dragon, Ox, Pig, Rat, and Tiger.

IF YOU ARE SAGITTARIUS BORN IN THE YEAR OF THE ROOSTER

酉

Years of the Rooster

1909	1957	2005	2053
1921	1969	2017	2065
1933	1981	2029	2077
1945	1993	2041	2089

The Rooster symbolizes courage, for in Asian mythology it rescued the Goddess of the Sun. Sincere and genuine, the Rooster has openhearted enthusiasm and a grand zest for life. This Rooster gusto blended with your Sagittarian boldness makes you doubly adventurous and extra resourceful. Your mind is razor-sharp, and you're most venturesome when exploring a subject other people pay little attention to. Some call you eccentric. It's true you have your foibles; you're disorganized and, curiously, both penny-pinching and extravagant, but you have genius-type skills. One of your great gifts is the ability to form lasting relationships—though your romantic affairs are not always happy, especially early on. You are very devoted, quite flirtatious, and demanding all at the same time. Later in life, you mellow out. Compatible partners are born in the Years of the Horse, Ox, and Snake.

Years of the Dog

1910	1958	2006	2054
1922	1970	2018	2066
1934	1982	2030	2078
1946	1994	2042	2090

Just as dogs are in real life, so the Chinese Dog is faithful and ever dependable. In Asia, the Dog is prized for its sense of duty. Dog practicality and being methodical combine with the Sagittarian unrestrained way of approaching ideas—making you a visionary thinker with a special bent for research. In general, you'd rather not step in front of huge audiences; you like one-on-one dealings and being left alone to do your thing. But you will stick your neck out to oppose anyone's actions that are unjust and mean-spirited. In a sense, you're on ethical guard duty. This quality of watchfulness is particularly apparent in love affairs. To begin with, you worry about rejection and take time to trust, and in general volatile emotions make you anxious. Ultimately, of course, you're completely faithful. Compatible partners are born in the Years of the Rabbit, Dog, Pig, and Tiger.

IF YOU ARE SAGITTARIUS BORN IN THE YEAR OF THE PIG

Years of the Pig

1911	1959	2007	2055
1923	1971	2019	2067
1935	1983	2031	2079
1947	1995	2043	2091

The pig tends to be an object of derision in the West, but the Asian Pig is gallant, chivalrous, and noble. A born intellectual as well as possessing an endearing sweetness, the Pig is loved for the confidence it gives to others. Pig strength and moral courage magnify your already expansive Sagittarian imagination, lending a superstar aura—although, modestly, you never seek the spotlight. It finds you, however, because your work has riveting style. People think fortune has forever smiled on you, but generally you start out having to suffer vicissitudes. Always, though, you're an achiever and quickly learn to enjoy the good life. You're a generous sharer and, in love, a great romantic. When you're smitten, you make a show of giving extravagant gifts and are a sexual voluptuary. Be careful about unscrupulous lovers taking advantage. Compatible partners are born in the Years of the Rabbit, Dog, Pig, and Tiger.

YOU AND NUMEROLOGY

Numerology is the language of numbers. It is the belief that there is a correlation between numbers and living things, ideas, and concepts. Certainly, numbers surround and infuse our lives (e.g., twenty-four hours in a day, twelve months of the year, etc.). And from ancient times mystics have taught that numbers carry a *vibration*, a deeper meaning that defines how each of us fits into the universe. According to numerology, you are born with a personal number that contains information about who you are and what you need to be happy. This number expresses what numerology calls your life path.

All numbers reduce to one of nine digits, numbers 1 through 9. Your personal number is based on your date of birth. To calculate your number, write your birth date in numerals. As an example, the birth date of November 25, 1982, is written 11-25-1982. Now begin the addition: 11 + 25 + 1 + 9 + 8 + 2 = 56; 56 reduces to 5 + 6 = 11; 11 reduces to 1 + 1 = 2. The personal number for someone born November 25, 1982, is *Two*.

IF YOU ARE A SAGITTARIUS ONE

Keywords: Confidence and Creativity

One is the number of leadership and new beginnings. You rush into whatever engages your heart—whether a new plan, a love affair, or just finding more pleasure. Courageous and inventive, you love larger-than-life experiences and hate the lulls. You're attracted to unusual creative pursuits because you like to stand out from the ordinary. You can't bear to be under the thumb of other people's whims and agendas. Careers that call to you are those in which you are in charge and able to work independently. As for love, you want ecstasy and passion, and the most exciting part of a flirtation is the beginning.

IF YOU ARE A SAGITTARIUS TWO

Keywords: Cooperation and Balance

Two is the number of cooperation and creating a secure entity. Being a Two gives you extra Sagittarian magnetism—you attract what you need. Your magic is not only your people skills, but also your ability to breathe life into empty forms (for example, a concept, an ambitious business idea, a new relationship) and produce something of worth. You're a gifted communicator—and because you have both a creative side *and* a practical side, you're drawn to careers that combine a business sense with an artistic challenge. In love, you want a companion of the heart, someone you can trust and share confidences with.

IF YOU ARE A SAGITTARIUS THREE

Keywords: Expression and Sensitivity

Three symbolizes self-expression. You have a gift for words and a talent for visualization. You link people together so that they benefit from each other. You stimulate others to think. Because you're a connector, you're much loved as a leader, spokesperson, and friend. In a career, Sagittarian creativity and innovation are your specialties. You're a quick study, mentally active, and curious about the new. In love, you need someone who excites you intellectually and sensually, and understands your complex personality. Casual acquaintances may not see your depth, but in love you must have a soulmate who does.

IF YOU ARE A SAGITTARIUS FOUR

Keywords: Stability and Process

Four is the number of dedication and loyalty. It represents *foundation*, exactly as a four-sided square does. You like to build, and the direction you go in is up. Sagittarius has a reputation for flying out in all directions, but you want to create something of value—and you have persistence. Therefore, you're able to accomplish great works. You look for self-expression in your craft, and are at your best when you can go at your own pace without others interfering. Sexually you're an imaginative and generous lover, and you need a giving and understanding partner with whom you can express your rich sensuality.

IF YOU ARE A SAGITTARIUS FIVE

Keywords: Freedom and Discipline

Five is the number of change and freedom. You're a gregarious nonconformist. With your chameleon intellect (it can go in any direction) and captivating ability to deal with people, you're a marvelous *persuader*. You charm and influence others, and have power with the public. In friendships, you're quick to jump in to give advice and whatever the other needs. Your deepest desire is to push past boundaries and express your free spirit. This is true sexually, as well, and you are a most inventive lover. But when you give your heart away for keeps it's to someone with whom you passionately mesh—body and mind.

IF YOU ARE A SAGITTARIUS SIX

Keywords: Vision and Acceptance

Six is the number of teaching, healing, and utilizing your talents. You're geared toward changing the world or at least fixing other people's lives. Being an advice-giver and even a therapist to your friends comes naturally. In addition, you're exacting—especially with yourself. You hold to high standards and bring an artisan's excellence to everything you do. *Six* carries humanitarian instincts, so you also bring uplifting energy to others. In love, you're fervent about being a helpmate and confidante. You're a true partner as well as a passionate sensualist who gives your all to someone you trust.

IF YOU ARE A SAGITTARIUS SEVEN

Keywords: Trust and Openness

Seven is the number of the mystic and the intensely focused specialist. You observe and, by analyzing, gain wisdom. You have an instinct for problem-solving, and in a flash understand how things work (in business, between people, etc.). You enjoy communicating your ideas and putting them to use. You're an intellectual and connoisseur of everything creative. You pursue *self*-determination (not being controlled by outside forces). At your core you're extremely loyal and intensely loving, though very selective about relationships. In love, your deepest need is for a partner who can help you in your life's journey.

IF YOU ARE A SAGITTARIUS EIGHT

Keywords: Abundance and Power

Eight is the number of mastery and authority. You are intelligent, alert, quick in action, and able to guide traffic into the direction you want. You work well with groups because you see what's needed and can delegate (a major success tool). You're also a good judge of character. Others sense you're the one who knows best, and they're right. As a Sagittarius Eight, you're likely to reach out to diversified groups, travel, and add to your education. Giving your promise in love is a serious act. You're a protective and caring lover, and in turn you need to know your lover is your loyal ally.

IF YOU ARE A SAGITTARIUS NINE

Keywords: Integrity and Wisdom

Nine is the path of the "old soul," the number of completion and full bloom. Because it's the last number, it sums up the highs and lows of human experience, and you live a life of dramatic events. People see you as colorful and heroic because you have an adventurous outlook but are also spiritual and altruistic. You're intellectual, interested in all kinds of exploration, do highly original work, and are an inspiration to others. In love, you're truthful and sincere—and also a romantic, sensual creature. As a Sagittarius Nine you generously give of yourself, often to the point of being sacrificing.

LAST WORD: YOUR SAGITTARIUS UNFINISHED BUSINESS

Psychologists often use the phrase *unfinished business* to describe unresolved issues—for example, patterns from childhood that cause unhappiness, anger that keeps one stuck, scenarios of family dysfunction that repeat through second and third generations (such as alcoholism or abusive behavior).

Astrology teaches that the past is indeed very much with us in the present—and that using astrological insights can help us to move out of emotional darkness into greater clarity. Even within this book (which is not a tome of hundreds of pages) you have read of many of the superlatives and challenges of being Sagittarius. You have breathtaking gifts and at the same time certain tendencies that can undermine utilizing these abilities.

In nature, a fascinating fact is that in jungles and forests a poisonous plant will grow in a certain spot, and always just a few feet away is a plant that is the antidote to that specific poison. Likewise, in astrology, the antidote is right there ready to be used when the negatives threaten to overwhelm your life.

Sagittarius's unfinished business has to do with *expansiveness*— your lovely quality of reaching for the stars. This is one of your best characteristics. It encourages you to strive and evolve, to be the best you can be. It connects you to your higher self and inspires others. The difficulty is when your unrestrained tendencies become "too much," and then too much becomes "never enough." Your inclination is to overdo—endless pursuit of pleasure, over-scheduling, nonstop socializing, gluttony, and excessive drinking, too many piles of unfinished projects. You're a profligate who fritters away precious time and energy. *Dissipation* is the negative aspect of expansion.

Caught up in the moment, you don't notice what's around you; your mind is far ahead. Your impulse is to soar, to be free of limitations, and so constraints such as time, schedules, and other people's expectations seem not to apply to you. Indeed, your sense of time is quite elastic. Your internal clock is always at least a half hour behind real time in the world, and you're forever running late. As for deadlines and time limits, you want to escape from these entirely. You adore leaping into a new venture, and do so with high hopes and sizable plans. But soon repetitive details and mind-dulling chores creep in, and you look for reasons to fly away. Sagittarius suffers from the Peter Pan syndrome—an unwillingness to take grown-up responsibility.

Sagittarius has enchanting childlike attributes (e.g., enthusiasm, joy in the moment) that, thwarted, can quickly turn childish. You become sulky, gloomy, and petulant, the way a child does when confronted with the word *no*. What you do take seriously are your frustrations, which make you angry. You're prone to falling into deep downers when life's realities clash with your magical thinking (the way you think your life should unfold).

Dogged discipline is not a Sagittarian trait. And when you lack discipline, you also lack direction, which easily leads to a dilettante approach of dabbling at this and then at that, and not becoming proficient at anything.

Procrastination also undoes you. You want to *enjoy*, and certainly don't want to put up with problems. The technique of avoidance is an easy escape. The results, however, are never easy, for in the end your talents lie by the wayside, unrealized and wasted. It isn't precisely that you're lazy—rather that you're self-indulgent. But the unfortunate result of too much self-indulgence is sloth.

You rely too much on luck and too little on the immutable principle of steady persistence—that day-by-day diligence will result in actually getting what, at the beginning, you wanted to get. Sagittarius doesn't pay much attention to the lesson of Aesop's fable of the Hare and the Tortoise.

Yet the antidotes are there to be found in their entirety in being Sagittarius, for you are the sign of *possibility*. You beam out the message that anything is achievable—and your optimism breaks down barricades. You're capable of creating opportunity where none existed.

The wonderful part about having big dreams is that embedded in them are big goals. When you concentrate your intelligence, use your time wisely, and stick to the *doing* of your endeavors, these goals become yours.

You're self-motivated, a rare quality. To you, life is a quest to explore what's on the horizon, and you operate from a sense of independence. Therefore, you don't need authority figures to motivate you; in fact, you rebel against anyone setting targets for you. *You're* the one who spurs you on.

You're also blessed with the ability to be happy! Being in your presence is uplifting; your infectious joy is one of the most precious gifts you give to others. Even when difficult problems assail, your nature is to rise above circumstances and find the meaning in what you're going through. A strong theme in the Sagittarian experience is the search for meaning. You're aware that there is a higher purpose, and are guided by lofty values. You're an idealist who is able to create a world that becomes a better place than you found it.

Astrologically, you come into this life with noble heritage. Much is bequeathed to you, and chief among your inborn treasures are foresight, flexibility, compassion, and a love of freedom and action. You have enthusiasm and vision. Like the Archer, symbol of your sign, you're a brave and gallant leader, and cosmic angels protect you.

FAMOUS PEOPLE WITH THE SUN IN SAGITTARIUS

Christina Aguilera
Louisa May Alcott
Woody Allen
Christina Applegate
Jane Austen
Tyra Banks
Kim Basinger
Ludwig van Beethoven
Busby Berkeley
William Blake
Kenneth Branagh
Leonid Brezhnev
Beau Bridges
Jeff Bridges
William F. Buckley
Hoagy Carmichael
Dale Carnegie
Winston Churchill
Dick Clark
Joseph Conrad
Noel Coward
Jamie Lee Curtis
Miley Cyrus
Sammy Davis Jr.
Emily Dickinson
Joan Didion
Charles de Gaulle
Joe DiMaggio
Walt Disney
Benjamin Disraeli
Kirk Douglas
Patty Duke
George Eliot

Chris Evert
Douglas Fairbanks Jr.
Jane Fonda
Lynn Fontanne
Jamie Foxx
Redd Foxx
Ira Gershwin
Margaret Hamilton
Ed Harris
Teri Hatcher
Jimi Hendrix
Abbie Hoffman
Katie Holmes
Jay-Z
Boris Karloff
John F. Kennedy Jr.
Billie Jean King
Fiorello La Guardia
Max Lerner
John Malkovich
David Mamet
Howie Mandel
Mary Martin
Harpo Marx
Margaret Mead
Bette Midler
John Milton
Carry Nation
Mandy Patinkin
Drew Pearson
Edith Piaf
Brad Pitt
Richard Pryor

Rainer Maria Rilke
Edward G. Robinson
Lillian Russell
William Safire
George Santayana
Charles Schulz
Eric Sevareid
Garry Shandling
Frank Sinatra
Margaret Chase Smith
Alexander Solzhenitsyn
Britney Spears
Steven Spielberg
Rex Stout
Jon Stewart
Kiefer Sutherland
Jonathan Swift
Michael Tilson Thomas
James Thurber
Henri de Toulouse-Lautrec
Tina Turner
Mark Twain
Cicely Tyson
Liv Ullmann
Dick Van Dyke
Gianni Versace
William Wegman
Rebecca West
Eli Whitney
John Greenleaf Whittier
Andy Williams
Flip Wilson

PART TWO

ALL ABOUT YOUR SIGN
OF SAGITTARIUS

SAGITTARIUS'S ASTROLOGICAL AFFINITIES, LINKS, AND LORE

SYMBOL: The Archer 🏹

Representing directness, high aims, love of outdoor activity and the chase, and a spiritual quest. Diana, the Roman goddess of the hunt, is linked to Sagittarius's Archer, underlining the themes of skill, grace, and being at one with the natural world. From ancient times, the Archer is not just any huntsman, but the mythical Centaur, the half-horse, half-man with his bow and arrow aimed toward heaven. The Centaur symbolizes the duality of being both a human being and a spiritual being.

RULING PLANET: Jupiter ♃

The most important Roman god, ruler of the heavens and king of the gods. The adjective "jovial" was originally used to describe people born under Jupiter, who were said to be jolly and buoyant in temperament. In astrology, Jupiter is the planet of good fortune, optimism, confidence, expansion, and abundance. It represents healing, help, and lucky protection.

DOMINANT KEYWORD

I SEE

GLYPH ↗

The pictograph represents the free-ranging, pointed arrow of the Archer aimed toward heaven. This is also a picture of the human leg from thigh to knee (the part of the anatomy that Sagittarius rules). In symbolic terms, it is the line of wisdom angled away from trouble and earthly concerns and pointing toward high ideals.

PART OF THE BODY RULED BY SAGITTARIUS:
The Liver, the Hips, and the Thighs

Sagittarius natives need lots of outdoor exercise in order to keep healthy. They have a sensitive liver and are susceptible to overuse of alcohol and to hepatitis.

LUCKY DAY: Thursday

The day named for Jupiter, ruler of Sagittarius. Our English word comes from the Norse, for Thor's Day. Thor, God of Thunder and the Sky, was the Anglo-Saxon version of Jupiter. The word for Thursday in romance languages, such as French and Spanish, comes from the Latin word *Joves*, meaning Jupiter.

LUCKY NUMBERS: 5 and 7

Numerologically, 5 is the number of growth, resourcefulness, vitality, and light—and 7 is linked to thinking, knowledge, and inner wisdom. These qualities align with the nature of Sagittarius.

TAROT CARD: Wheel of Fortune

The card in the Tarot linked to Sagittarius is the Wheel of Fortune. An ancient name for this card is Lord of the Forces of Life. In the Tarot, this card signifies the ups and downs of fate and the life cycles that go around and around. It speaks of the force that continually draws us on the path of our destiny. When this card turns up in a Tarot reading, this card points to new conditions about to arrive that will require adaptability—and also says that events ahead may be chaotic at first, but gradually a clear pattern will emerge leading to the end result.

The card itself pictures a wheel with the letters TARO in it, and in the four corners of the card are symbols of the four Fixed signs of the zodiac. The wheel represents life ever-turning against the background of fixed reality.

For Sagittarius, the Wheel of Fortune tells you to be alert to opportunity and face change with courage. All that will unfold in your life and the missions you must fulfill will arrive at the right time.

MAGICAL BIRTHSTONE: Turquoise

A gemstone prized for its unique color and use as a talisman. The word turquoise comes from the French word, *turques*, meaning "Turkish," for the finest gems were mined in Turkey. Because turquoise is affected by changes in body temperature, it was thought to indicate the health of the wearer. For thousands of years, turquoise has been known as a healing stone and bringer of good fortune. In Aztec, Mayan, and Native American cultures, turquoise was called "stone of the gods" and believed to ward off the Evil Eye. For Sagittarius, turquoise is said to attract love, protect from harm, and give its wearer the ability to see into the future.

SPECIAL COLOR: Purple

Uncommon color of royalty and the artistic. Kings, emperors, and powerful members of the clergy (such as bishops) wear purple to show their rank. Purple signifies power, majesty, and all things splendid.

CONSTELLATION OF SAGITTARIUS

Sagittarius is the Latin word for archer, and this constellation is commonly represented as a centaur drawing a bow. The Babylonians called this constellation *Pabilsag*, who was a centaur-like god firing an arrow from a bow, and known as Wise Being and Chief Ancestor. In Roman mythology, Sagittarius was the revered figure of Chiron, wisest of centaurs who brought to humankind gifts of medicine and healing. In the zodiac, the arrow of Sagittarius points toward the star Antares, the "Heart of the Scorpion." Thus, Sagittarius symbolizes victory over death (dark ignorance) through spiritual enlightenment.

CITIES

Budapest, Cologne, Toledo, Acapulco

COUNTRIES

Spain, Hungary, Australia, South Africa

FLOWERS

Narcissus, Holly, and Dandelion

TREES

Mulberry, Oak, Birch, and Lime

HERBS AND SPICES

Balsam, Sage, Aniseed, and Lemon Balm

METAL: Tin

A silvery, malleable metal often combined with other metals. The mining and use of tin dates back to the Bronze Age, around 3000 B.C. Tin is used to coat other metals, such as bronze and copper, to prevent their corrosion. Plus, its addition to other metals makes casting and molding of the metals far easier. Thus, tin symbolizes improvement and flexibility, qualities that align with Sagittarius.

ANIMALS RULED BY SAGITTARIUS

Horses in particular, and animals (such as deer) that are hunted

DANGER

Sagittarians are subject to accidents of fire and explosion, especially while traveling. Their strong desire for freedom may also incite jealousy and possessiveness on the part of a lover.

PERSONAL PROVERBS

Every day is a new beginning. Stay away from what might have been, and look at what can be.

In the long run, you can hit only what you aim at.

KEYWORDS FOR SAGITTARIUS

Expansive
Lucky
High-spirited
Optimistic
Always in motion
Adventurous
Extravagant
Generous
Honest and trustworthy
Truthful and blunt
Independent
Progressive
Visionary
Charming
Adaptable
Philosophical
Spiritually minded
Versatile
Slapdash
Disorganized

Impulsive
Gullible
Impulsive
Overconfident
Feels intellectually superior
Exhibitionist

HOW ASTROLOGY SLICES AND DICES YOUR SIGN OF SAGITTARIUS

DUALITY: Masculine

The twelve astrological signs are divided into two groups, *masculine* and *feminine*. Six are masculine and six are feminine; this is known as the sign's *duality*. A masculine sign is direct and energetic. A feminine sign is receptive and magnetic. These attributes were given to the signs about 2,500 years ago. Today modern astrologers avoid the sexism implicit in these distinctions. A masculine sign does not mean "positive and forceful" any more than a feminine sign means "negative and weak." In modern terminology, the masculine signs, such as your sign of Sagittarius, are defined as outer-directed and strong through action. The feminine signs are self-contained and strong through inner reserves.

TRIPLICITY (ELEMENT): Fire

The twelve signs are also divided into groups of three signs each. These three-sign groups are called a *triplicity*, and each of these denotes an *element*. The elements are *Fire*, *Earth*, *Air*, and *Water*. In astrology, an element symbolizes a fundamental characterization of the sign.

The three *Fire* signs are Aries, Leo, and Sagittarius. Fire signs are active and enthusiastic.

The three *Earth* signs are Taurus, Virgo, and Capricorn. Earth signs are practical and stable.

The three *Air* signs are Gemini, Libra, and Aquarius. Air signs are intellectual and communicative.

The three *Water* signs are Cancer, Scorpio, and Pisces. Water signs are emotional and intuitive.

QUADRUPLICITY (QUALITY): Mutable

The twelve signs are also divided into groups of four signs each. These four-sign groups are called a *quadruplicity*, and each of these denotes a *quality*. The qualities are *Cardinal*, *Fixed*, and *Mutable*. In astrology, the quality signifies the sign's interaction with the outside world.

Four signs are *Cardinal** signs. They are Aries, Cancer, Libra, and Capricorn. Cardinal signs are enterprising and outgoing. They are the initiators and leaders.

*When the Sun crosses the four cardinal points in the zodiac, we mark the beginning of each of our four seasons. Aries begins spring; Cancer begins summer; Libra begins fall; Capricorn begins winter.

Four signs are *Fixed*. They are Taurus, Leo, Scorpio, and Aquarius. Fixed signs are resistant to change. They hold on; they're perfectors and finishers rather than originators.

Four signs are *Mutable*. They are Gemini, Virgo, Sagittarius, and Pisces. Mutable signs are flexible, versatile, and adaptable. They are able to adjust to differing circumstances.

Your sign of Sagittarius is a Masculine, Fire, Mutable sign—and no other sign in the zodiac is this exact combination. Your sign is a one-of-a-kind combination, and therefore you express the characteristics of your duality, element, and quality differently from any other sign.

For example, your sign is a *Masculine* sign, meaning you are active, outgoing, highly motivated. You're a *Fire* sign, meaning you're enthusiastic, energetic, and courageous. And you're a *Mutable* sign, meaning you're able to go with the flow, adjust, and quickly adapt to new situations.

Now the sign of Aries is also Masculine and Fire, but unlike Sagittarius (which is Mutable), Aries is Cardinal. Like you, Aries is a passionate go-getter with a positive outlook who pursues ambitious goals—but Aries is invested in being the leader. Aries initiates and is caught up in new beginnings. Its motivation is to be the locomotive, the one in front driving the enterprise, and doesn't have your adaptability. You, being Mutable, have an exploratory nature that wants to take the road less traveled. The destination is less important than the journey. You're a seeker of knowledge and the unusual adventure—and your motivation is to gain the freedom to go where the flow takes you.

Leo, too, is Masculine and Fire, but unlike Sagittarius (which is Mutable), Leo is Fixed. Like you, Leo has drive and courage and a generous heart, and you share the qualities of exuberance and bringing a vivacious cheeriness to others. However, being Fixed, Leo is adamant, unwilling to compromise, and can get mired in its own ego. Leo doesn't have your flexibility, especially when it comes to letting go of a pet opinion (an *idée fixe*) and moving on to other options. You, on the other hand, are Mutable, and the last thing you want is to be stuck. Your restless nature avoids the immovable. Often called the enthusiastic philosopher, you have an open mind. You see the bigger picture and are fond of change, and your goal is to discover.

POLARITY: Gemini

The twelve signs are also divided into groups of two signs each. These two-sign groups are called a *polarity* (meaning "opposite"). Each sign in the zodiac has a polarity, which is its opposite sign in the other half of the zodiac. The two signs express opposite characteristics.

Sagittarius and Gemini are a polarity. Sagittarius is the sign of freedom, higher learning, and broad concepts. The themes of exploring distant places and aspiring to lofty goals run through your life. You're the sign of idealism, journeys of the mind and body, unearthing new experiences, and exploring different ways of thinking. On a spiritual level, Sagittarius represents moral ethics, the unfolding of inner wisdom, and expansion of consciousness.

You are born with wanderlust, mentally and physically, and you move with the winds of change. Your instinct is to rise above the petty and aspire to something with greater meaning. You're spurred by a sense of mission and try not to get tied down with personal commitments. To be Sagittarius means you're never at home in the minutiae of ordinary life—you're most alive when leaping toward a new horizon.

Gemini, your opposite sign, is the sign of personal expression and communicating one-on-one. It rules daily encounters, mental acuity, and the dissemination of news and information. Gemini people are extremely verbal and gregarious, love to give advice, and tend to integrate themselves into others' lives. Marked characteristics are curiosity, versatility, quick-wittedness, and being able to analyze precisely. Gemini represents the essentially human trait of making connections—and among its nicest qualities is a willingness to jump in to bring cheer and support.

Astrologically, you as a Sagittarian can benefit from adopting some of Gemini's immediacy. Gemini lives in the now; Sagittarius can be so future-oriented that many details don't get handled in the present. A Sagittarian pitfall is wasting time, energy, and brainpower on an unrealistic pursuit, which not only keeps you discontented but, in fact, stuck. You tend to see your own desires as "truths" that you have a calling to accomplish, whereas they may only be grandiose notions.

Another worthy aspect to adopt from Gemini is its strong links to its immediate environment of friendships, acquaintances, and social life. You have a more no-strings attitude. Sagittarius struggles with conflict around closeness—which isn't to say you're not extremely loving and loyal. It's that your basic drive is to fly outward and experience an expansive life. On a certain psychological level you feel trapped by ties that bind. It would serve you to feel instead that your close connections are the wind beneath your wings.

In turn, Gemini has lessons to learn from you, among them to lift its eyes to the more important. Gemini tends to overcomplicate daily life with too much busyness, too many commitments it can't fulfill, not knowing how to prioritize time, being disorganized. Gemini's mind whirls around distractedly.

You take a more removed approach to small crises. Your detachment makes day-to-day chaos easier to handle and to view as only one small piece of the whole. You are wise, philosophical, kind, and humanitarian. You see the passing scene with a hard-to-extinguish *joie de vivre* and always look for the positive something that makes the future promising. The best part is that you're busy expanding your knowledge and learning about people and the world around you.